I AM

An Unchanging God
in a
World of Change

Beth Weikel

by His design Publishing

I AM is written by Beth Weikel
Copyright © 2009, Beth Weikel
Photographs Copyright © 2009, Beth Weikel

Published and printed by:

by His design Publishing

445C East Cheyenne Mtn. Blvd. # 139
Colorado Springs, Co 80906
byhisdesignonline.com
lifefromloss.com

Printed in the United States of America

ISBN 978-0-9825361-1-7

Dedication

To David, my fellow traveler on this road to finding more of Him. Your patience, support, encouragement, and tireless use of your talents make me want to continue the climb. We are loved because He first loved us.

Table of Contents

Introduction

Jesus, More than Enough

"Learning to be and not to do, Savior, lead me"

The gospels are full of Jesus' example, a life lived flawlessly before God and men. Because we know the victorious outcome, it seems to us that He made it look almost easy. He's God, so what's the real problem? Jesus always knew the right thing to do.

But the real lesson is before and after the "doing." Notice the "being" times. In the being, Jesus gained renewed vision and strength. Without fanfare, He spent time apart in the Father's presence, seeking His face, aligning His will. These are the silent periods the gospel writers could only outline for us. When Jesus did speak or perform His miraculous deeds, it was because of His dependence on the Father and His plan. Never in a hurry, knowing how to respond—with gentleness and mercy, insight or a well-timed rebuke, Jesus lived a life of purpose, deliberately. In humility, giving glory to the Father, He never faltered.

Those that desire to follow Him, not just His example, will need to do the same. The aim of this study is to explore the claims Jesus made in the Gospel of John on a personal level and access the power and intention of each in order to let the Holy Spirit transform us by their truth. So as life presents itself, with all the confusion and challenges that we experience in a world of uncertainty, we can be filled with Jesus in a fresh way, addressing the need of the moment. No formulas, just the Son of God, as the Father intended. His pathways become our pathways; His power, love, and truth lived out as we single-mindedly allow the Spirit to guide us through every trial and test of character.

How to use this study

This study should be done each day through the week. Each "I Am" statement should take one week to complete, with each day taking between 15-30 min. to complete. On the **first day,** **"Ground Work,"** do the preview reading of the Scripture reference, study the picture and read through the prayer(s) as a devotional reading, preparing your heart to hear what the Scripture passage says. Space is provided to record your initial observations and impressions of the visual, as well as the prayer(s). The **second day's** reading, "Faith Walk," will include a real-life illustration of the "I Am" and will be followed by the reading of the entire Scripture passage. Space is provided to record your thoughts and feelings as you connect your "story" to the example given. On the **third and fourth days,** "Truth Dig," work through the Bible study section designed to reveal the significance of the "I Am" in context and also in relation to the whole counsel of God's Word. Give yourself the privilege of being in an intimate place with God. Take time to study, as well as listen to what the Spirit is teaching you. Finally, on **day five,** "Now What...?" complete the application portion and journal your own prayer. By this time God's voice should be evident, as He reassures you of His love and guides you further down the path with Him. Each "I Am" statement will follow this same pattern for nine weeks. The Epilogue and Appendices A-C will also provide additional material that allows you to explore in more depth how to live with this new reality of letting Jesus be more than enough when life overwhelms.

Chapter One
Jesus' Deity
Read John 1: 1-18

Jesus... the Word,

Creator, Eternal

Jesus, the Word

John 1

Eternal, unerring Son of the Most High,

speak your creation power into my barren, dumb places.

Renew my fallen mind with precious communion,

dissolving dark threats, dispelling crafty lies.

Life-giver, Light-shiner,

replace stalking fear with pure faith.

Speak until I behold your true Self,

full of glory, grace, and truth,

revealing God to this weary soul.

Day One: Ground Work

Record your initial observations and impressions of both the visual and the prayer:

How are they related to the Scripture reading?

How are these elements preparing your heart to hear God's message to you? (What need are you aware of?)

Day Two: Faith Walk

Deity-

To accept Jesus' deity, one must believe the Scriptures that proclaim Him as the benevolent controller of all things, the One who creates order, and knows no impossibilities.

I once wrote an article called, "My Life as Whirligig." Unless you are a fan of Folk Art, you may not appreciate this curious piece of Americana. Whirligigs are hand-crafted from wood and represent the diligence and simplicity of the Yankee work ethic. I first became aware of them while touring New England one summer. We saw these brightly painted figures dancing in the breeze on the side of the road—tradesmen, fishermen, farmers, housewives all doing their chores with abandon, as long as the wind propelled them. I brought home a fine example of a woodsman cutting his yearly cord of firewood for the harsh New England winters.

My tireless friend found life in the Rocky Mts. suitable enough. I could see him easily from my kitchen window and enjoyed knowing that we were both productive and busy providing necessary things. One day after an unpredictable spring blow, however, he was nowhere to be found. Venturing into the backyard, it was all too apparent what must have happened. He was lying sprawled on the ground in pieces—feet detached from his platform, gears disassembled, and his pinwheel missing most of its paddles.

I bent over the wreckage to collect as much as I could to transfer to my husband's workbench for repair. But en route a curious thing happened. My Lord spoke to my own condition, "That's you," I heard whispered to my heart. It was true; we also were in the midst of a fierce season of storms and merciless gales. Life, as we planned, was coming apart. Time to stop and assess the damage: health threats, surgery and treatment endured; the loss of close family members, one after another in quick succession, some anticipated, but some not; now relationships strained under the load were fraying. There seemed to be no end in sight.

As I placed the small figure and his entourage of splintered puzzle pieces in the garage with the hopes that with some skillful care, glue, refastening, and even creative restoration, that delightful reminder of New England fortitude would once again take his place in my garden. My Maker's promises are no less reason for hope.

"Do not be surprised at the fiery ordeal that overtakes you… When the flood comes, you will not be overcome… Persecuted, but not forsaken… Always carrying about the dying of Jesus, that the life of Jesus… "

At times like these I need Deity, a God like no other: holy and pure, so that I can trust Him and His words; historically selfless in His love for me; One with everlasting, almighty, legendary power; and most especially, a sovereign God who has a plan, not a hunch, not good intentions, but a sure thing. Only that kind of God is adequate for this time.

I, along with many others I'm sure, am tired of deceit, broken promises, manipulation, rip-offs, and whatever else humans are capable of. I'm also weary of so-called happenstance, those shocking episodes that defy explanation. So, if today's headlines are coming a little too close for comfort, find out about this one-of-a-kind Source of life, no matter the circumstances. Give Him your splintered puzzle pieces and spend time with Him;

there's really no other cure, and everything else depends on it. His skillful care and creative restoration merely await our yielded posture of relinquishment. When life takes its toll, and there's only enough energy left to surrender, only then will you find a more-than-enough Jesus.

Read John 1: 1-18

What did you notice the second time you read this passage that you didn't the first time?

What part of the real-life example spoke to you?

What thoughts and feelings came to mind?

How is this related to something you've walked through? Or are currently walking with?

Days Three and Four: Truth Dig --facts and lessons

Why Is He Deity?

John 1: 1-18

Starting with this passage, we can grasp the wonder of Jesus. These verses answer the question – Who, in your opinion, is Jesus? Most would probably say that He is the Son of God. But how do we know He is? John gives us four reasons why.

John 1: 1-2 Jesus is eternal

1. Is John saying that there is a beginning to eternity (In the Beginning)?

2. Who is the Word? How do you know? (see also John 17:5, 1:14)

3. What does Psalm 90: 1-2 say about eternity?

4. Describe eternity in reference to Jesus. (See also Col. 1:17)

John 1:3-5, 9 Jesus as Creator

1. Who is the creator? (see also Col. 1:16)

2. Why does John use "came into being" three times in verse 3?

3. Is every man enlightened?

4. Can darkness pervade light? Can there be light without life?

John 1: 10 – 17 Jesus dwelt among us

1. Why is it important to understand that Jesus came in the flesh?

2. How could the world not know Him?

3. What happens when you receive Him? How does this happen? (verses 12-13)

4. When Jesus became flesh what did we learn about Him?

5. According to Mark 14: 61-62, Jesus is answering before a court of His accusers. What question did the high priest put to Him?

When Jesus replies, "I am," what is He referring to?

Why was this answer interpreted as "blasphemy?" (see Mk. 14: 63-64)

John 1: 1-18   Jesus, the Word, explains God

    1. How did Jesus explain God to us?

What does this mean to me? Tell in your own words
what each of the four points are:

Which one is easiest for you to accept?

Which one is the most difficult?

Ask God to help you view Jesus in each of these four
ways, more and more, as you go through the pages
of this study. Be open to the creative methods He
employs.

Day Five: Now What...?

What promise, desire, warning, command, or word of encouragement are you to pay attention to?

What action will you take --today? (Even if it's to "wait"). Record what you did about it.

-- and how God is working.

What do you need from Him?

Life Response -- Briefly explain why these verses
are important to you? Try phrasing your answer in
"I Am" statements (like the prayer on Day One) by
recording your need and how Jesus' deity can meet
that need, regardless of your doubts. Acknowledge
these doubts and replace them with the points of truth
you just learned. Meditate on this, your personal
prayer to God. Use it whenever the need arises to
remind yourself of what you're learning through
experience and trust, regardless of the size of the trial.

Write your prayer out, sign and date it. Let it be a covenant between your Lord and you.

Chapter Two

Living Water

Read John 4: 1-26

I Am
the
Living
Water

Son of God, Living Water

John 4, 7:38

I'm so thirsty in this dry land.

I come to You with hands cupped, head back.

Gift of God, give me Your deep well,

Your everlasting spring.

Hydrate my parched places, my very soul.

Flood my being with Your refreshing Presence.

Day One: Ground Work

Record your initial observations and impressions of both the visual and the prayer:

How are they related to the Scripture reading?

How are these elements preparing your heart to hear God's message to you? (What need are you aware of?)

Day Two: Faith Walk

Living Water-

There was a time both in ministry and while teaching adolescents (often at the same time), I can attest to dry periods: alone in the desert wandering, bone-sucking wasteland experiences, give-my–life-for-a –taste-of-pure-refreshment arid times! Been there? Fortunately, these weren't the norm.

Since I'm not a flaming extrovert, the intensity of these callings drained my reserves in short order. Wanting to reach out and be effective, seeing these opportunities as a privilege but knowing that my natural gifts wouldn't allow me to just cruise in these waters, I could find myself overwhelmed. With people come problems; the more people, the more problems: personality conflicts, unrealistic demands, time pressure, the lack of follow-through, and so many others.

Admitting that one is helpless and in need is a good first step. Knowing my condition and refusing to spin my wheels is progress. Looking back, though, I think the commonality of these episodes was that I was looking for water in the wrong places: unburdening myself during a break with a colleague, coming home to an equally weary spouse and asking for sympathy and some perspective, escaping in front of TV or some other amusement are all helpful to a point, but don't begin to touch the depths of these times of continual energy (emotional, physical, and mental)outlay. The well is running dry. After the striving, panic, desperation, and complaining, I usually figured out that Someone bigger should be consulted. Living Water, not the constant drip…drip… of daily life.

The Bible describes many forms of satisfying, as well as terrifying water experiences. Think of some picturesque words to describe the properties of water and why we crave it so. A daily application of water is that it cleanses and refreshes. Few other things do. It moves and fascinates, appealing even to look at.

Sometimes what I needed was the constant mist of a spring shower in a cool glade out of the glaring sun. Other times, just the soothing sound of a mountain stream tumbling over smooth stones on its way to a placid pool would relieve. Or even the surging power of a majestic waterfall flooding my senses, lifting my spirit was exactly the solution to my feeling inadequate. Running dry? Longing for refreshment? What type? Can Jesus really meet these very different needs? The Maker, originator of water, itself, Who knows your own exact dry place? He is an ocean of satisfaction, hydrating the soul of the overwhelmed.

In Genesis 21: 9-21, Hagar and her son, Ishmael, found themselves in such a dry, desperate place. Abraham's wife Sarah had used Hagar to expedite God's promise to them, but then didn't like the result. So, after a time Hagar and Ishmael were taken out into the desert wilderness with a few provisions. As expected, they soon became destitute. Hagar then left her son under one of the bushes and went a little ways away, "not wanting to see her son die." And as they both cried piteously, God heard (because He hadn't lost notice of them at any time), whereupon He sent an angel saying, "Do not fear…" and gave her an amazing promise that He would make of her son a great nation. Finally, it was then that God opened her eyes to see a well of water nearby. But the real lesson was that God was their source of life, hope and refreshing. It was not a matter of geography; though He could have picked them out of the desert and planted them at the seashore, He chose not to. No, they continued to live in the wilderness, but now in God's presence with purpose and provision.

Read John 4: 1-26

What did you notice the second time you read this passage that you didn't the first time?

What part of the real-life example spoke to you?

What thoughts and feelings came to mind?

How is this related to something you've walked through? Or are currently walking with?

Days Three and Four:
Truth Dig—facts and lessons

I Am Living Water

John 4: 1-26

Jesus is taking the time to teach a Samaritan woman about living water. This water is eternal and available. It is Jesus. While being wearied from his journey, Jesus, Himself, uses the word "thirst," but is referring to humanity and its needs, not just the result of traveling in an arid region. In studying this Scripture, we will see that Jesus is proclaiming that He meets these needs through who He is, if we drink of Him.

John 4: 1-9   Jesus speaks to a sinner

1. It is significant that Jesus is at the ancient site of Jacob's well. Why do Jews and the Samaritans dislike, even detest each other?

2. Why would Jesus talk to a woman?

3. Notice that Jesus never misses an opportunity. How does Jesus approach the Samaritan woman?

John 4: 10-14   Jesus' promise

1. Why would it make a difference if the woman
    knew who Jesus was, as the Christ?

2. What is Jesus referring to here in the area of
    thirst (think spiritually)?

3. If the woman drank of Jesus, she would never
    thirst. What are the two things Jesus promises
    and what does each mean spiritually?

John 4: 15-18   The woman exposed

1. Why would Jesus expose the woman's life?

2. How did this prepare her to hear the truth?

John 4: 19-26   Jesus is Living Water

1. Why is Jesus talking about worship and where to worship?

2. What does Jesus mean that salvation is from the Jews?

3. How do you worship in Spirit and in Truth? (verses 20-24, Romans 12: 1-2, Heb. 11:6, Ps 51:6, 10-17)

4. The woman knows about the Christ to come. Jesus says He is the Christ. Jesus says He is the Living Water. What is He saying to her?

What does this mean to me? When have you been
aware of spiritual thirst? Describe this.

How has Jesus been Living Water to you, met your
thirst? Give some examples.

(See also Jeremiah 2:13, Psalm 23:1-3, Psalm 107:
33-43, Revelation 22: 17, 20-21). Take time to record
your feelings and the truths that you are learning.

Pray and ask Jesus to refresh you with Himself today.
Come to the well that is promised to anyone who thirsts.
Stay there as long as needed to let Him revive you.

What is He saying about your lifestyle? Are you
settling for broken cisterns that cannot hold water, or
are you a true worshiper?

Are you weary and ready now never to be thirsty
again, because His well never runs dry? (verse 14)

Day Five: Now What...?

What promise, desire, warning, command, or word of encouragement are you to pay attention to?

What action will you take --today? (Even if it's to "wait"). Record what you did about it.

-- and how God is working.

What do you need from Him?

Life Response -- Briefly explain why these verses are important to you? Try phrasing your answer in "I Am" statements (like the prayer on Day One) by recording your need and how The Living Water can meet that need, regardless of your doubts. Acknowledge these doubts and replace them with the points of truth you just learned. Meditate on this, your personal prayer to God. Use it whenever the need arises to remind yourself of what you're learning through experience and trust, regardless of the size of the trial.

Write your prayer out, sign and date it. Let it be a covenant between your Lord and you.

Chapter Three

Bread of Life

Read John 6: 22-71

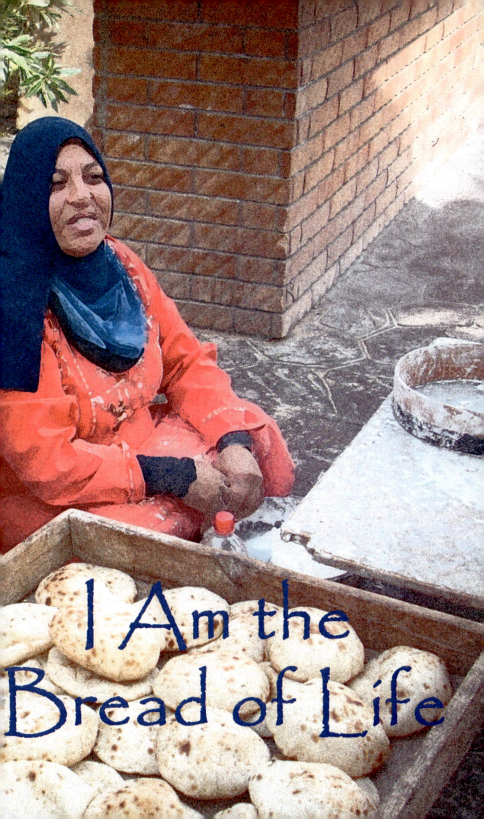

I Am the
Bread of Life

Jesus, Bread of Life

John 6: 35, 48

Giver of daily sustenance for all my hunger.

Abundant provision every day,

filling the appetite of fear and doubt.

Yours is the only food from heaven.

Bread of God,

give life to me and through me.

Make me strong;

feed me with Your wholeness, Your true body,

eternally.

Bread of Life II

Mysterious Manna in my wilderness,
Heavenly Source,
Satisfy.
Let me not grumble… argue… stumble;
But, like Peter,
Know
--the Holy One of God.
Draw me to your own Self
and raise me up, Father,
<u>Believing.</u>
Teach me to feed on real food,
Living Bread,
And remain with you, forever.
Your Flesh, Lord, given for me,
true food,
Abiding in the One who came out of heaven,
Your Words, your Spirit, Your Life.
Heavenly Source,
Satisfy.
Mysterious Manna in my wilderness…

Day One: Ground Work

Record your initial observations and impressions of
both the visual and the prayer:

How are they related to the Scripture reading?

How are these elements preparing your heart to hear
God's message to you? (What need are you aware of?)

Day Two: Faith Walk

Bread-

Not many in First-World countries know true starvation.
In our society most of Americans are plagued by a
different form of hunger—the gnawing of dissatisfaction,
real sustenance, a vague apprehension that something is
missing. Often we live this way until real crisis develops.
In my case it was a life-threatening illness at the worst
possible time.

I was a brand new grandmother of a darling two-month-
old who lived in another state. My husband and I
were reveling in this new phase of life and anticipating
retirement in a few years where we could relax our
schedules and see where this new adventure called
"grandparenting" would take us.

It was the start of a new school year, and I was
enthusiastically developing a special curriculum for high
schoolers. I took advantage of a break to call the women's
clinic for an appointment to check out something and was
starting to feel annoyed that they couldn't work around my
teaching schedule. Getting a sub just meant more work
with less results. So, after getting an ultrasound, on their
terms, I found myself waiting in the doctor's office for the
radiologist's report and wondering what the delay was.
The next thing I remember was hearing these words, "You
have a mass…" from the sober-faced doctor, who wouldn't
let me leave the examination room without a follow-up
appointment. What followed was a series of disruptions in
more lives than my own. Serious illness can do that. One
moment we think we are in charge of our responsibilities
and schedules, and the next we are anything but.

After treatment ended months later, I was home on medical
leave anticipating early retirement from education. My
days were unstructured compared to before, but I had
an agenda: workouts, nutrition, rest, and Bible study
times with my Lord. It was during these weeks and
months that I learned what it meant to be "loved with
an everlasting love," and be fed manna every day. God
gave me His daily bread in the form of sweet expressions
of encouragement and love from so many others that I
knew I would never be the same. Some of these were
from unlikely sources, even strangers. He also kept our
daily appointments centered around my Bible reading,
journaling, and prayer. I can't give a formula for this; I
just sat in a comfortable place bathed in sunlight taking
in daily doses of wisdom, from a Godly perspective,
and strength, from His many promises and words of
reassurance, until I knew I was full for that time. It was
a precious experience of walking in step, trusting in His
care. As I availed myself of this opportunity, the message
from Him was clear, "I love you, really and truly." The
implication from my head to my heart was, "never doubt
this again."

What are you hungering for, starving for? So much of this
life promises fulfillment, but like fast food, leaves one on
empty, malnourished, still looking for satisfaction.

Read John 4: 1-26

What did you notice the second time you read this passage that you didn't the first time?

What part of the real-life example spoke to you?

What thoughts and feelings came to mind?

How is this related to something you've walked through? Or are currently walking with?

Days Three and Four:
Truth Dig —facts and lessons

I Am the Bread of Life

John 6: 22-71

A great miracle had occurred previous to this
passage. The Lord fed some followers by showing
deep care for them so that they were full, which was
very unusual for people at this time. They woke
up the next morning and were hungry again, even
though they had stuffed themselves. The drive of
the multitude is to eat and be full again. Jesus has a
better way.

John 6: 22-26 Seeking Jesus

1.   Why doesn't Jesus answer the question
     – "Rabbi, when did you get here?"

2.   Why did He say what He said to them?

3.   Do you think they were seeking Him because He
     could feed them or was there something else?

John 6: 27-36 Jesus, the Bread of Life

1. Jesus compares food that perishes with meat that endures. What is His reason for making this comparison?

2. What are the two methods of filling the appetite?

3. Why do they want another sign?

4. When you read Exodus 16: 15-35 you get an understanding of manna. Why would they believe that Moses gave them manna?

5. Why didn't they believe that Jesus was the Bread of Life?

John 6: 37-46 The Father's gift

    1. What is the Father's role in salvation?

John 6: 47-58 The promise

    1. In this passage what are the promises of God?

What does this mean to me? Apply this Scripture to own your life. What is God teaching you? Note all the dimensions of this personal application. What facets of hunger are you aware of that He can meet only with His supernatural love and abilities?

Then write that out. You may start by praising Jesus for being who He is and confessing your need of Him. Trusting Him before you see evidence of blessing is called "faith" and you can thank Him for supplying what He knows will satisfy you.

Agree with God in what He wants you to do about this, then trust Him to accomplish it through you by His grace, as you continue to look to Him daily.

Day Five: Now What...?

What promise, desire, warning, command, or word of
encouragement are you to pay attention to?

What action will you take --today? (Even if it's to
"wait"). Record what you did about it.

-- and how God is working.

What do you need from Him?

Life Response -- Briefly explain why these verses
are important to you? Try phrasing your answer
in "I Am" statements (like the prayer on Day One)
by recording your need and how The Bread of
Life can meet that need, regardless of your doubts.
Acknowledge these doubts and replace them with
the points of truth you just learned. Meditate on this,
your personal prayer to God. Use it whenever the
need arises to remind yourself of what you're learning
through experience and trust, regardless of the size of
the trial.

Write your prayer out, sign and date it. Let it be a covenant between your Lord and you.

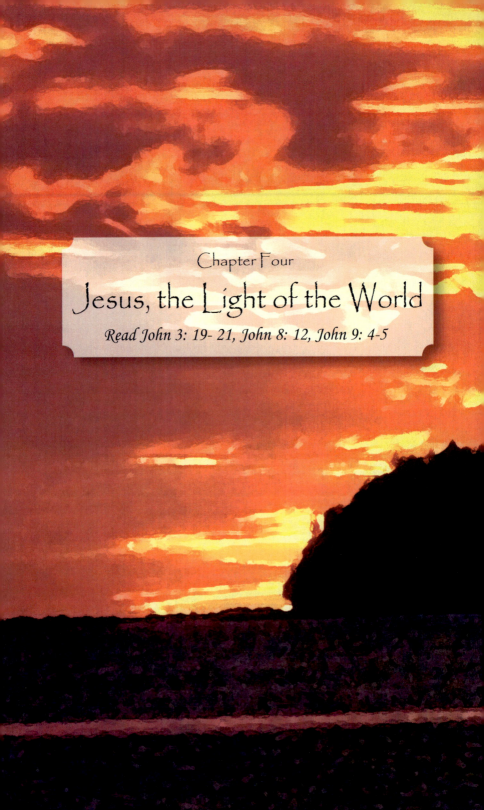

Chapter Four

Jesus, the Light of the World

Read John 3: 19- 21, John 8: 12, John 9: 4-5

I Am the Light

Jesus, the light of the world

John 3: 19-21, 8:12, 9:4-5

...Take me from this dark place of groping about,

grasping for hand-holds of dawn.

Make me follow the brightness of Your holiness

and take hold of the steady beacon leading to understanding.

Will me to see You, believe You,

and draw ever nearer to the light that keeps me from stumbling.

Make me blaze in Your presence.

Day One: Ground Work

Record your initial observations and impressions of both the visual and the prayer:

How are they related to the Scripture reading?

How are these elements preparing your heart to hear God's message to you? (What need are you aware of?)

Day Two: Faith Walk

Light-

In my new "retired" life, apart from a career, I accepted
opportunities to reach out and learn. One such group that
welcomed me was an international ministry to women
living in the U.S. A group of us volunteers would spend
time monthly with internationals from all parts of the
world. We met in a church, but these women were not
usually Christ followers. They often had survival English
language skills or none of any consequence. We would
start with food, which translates into community in any
language, and move into getting to know each other as best
we could, then listening to an inspirational talk that could
include very practical information, and finally working
with our hands on a craft to take home amid much laughter
and fun. We have also developed more specialized outings
between these formal meetings to include knitting circles,
hiking, cooking international dishes, lunch at a local ethnic
restaurant, English as a second language and Bible study
classes.

After months of this, I was asked to be the inspirational
speaker for December. It was decided that I would
introduce a clip from the new film release, *The Nativity*,
which meant I wouldn't be saying much. Our evangelistic
methods were stealthy at best. We respected the women
and their beliefs, but also wanted to give them an
understanding of ours. We wanted them to have the
opportunity to embrace the God we loved. After prayer
and listening, I prepared to speak about the God of Light in
this season of lights. Jesus came to give man His light and
illumine the darkness that surrounds us on all sides. He
came to a society and a world not much different than our

own, pre-occupied with politics and power while offering few real solutions to the suffering of so many.

Mary and Joseph, a very young couple, obeyed the voice of God and walked in His light. In spite of their feelings and reservations, they agreed to be used by God to fulfill His promise made down through the ages. Jesus, the Light of the World, whose birth we celebrate each December with our decorated trees, the lights we put on our houses, our candlelight services, and the carols we sing, came to us to shine the truth of the good news into the dark of men, women, and children's hearts. God's only Son, given in love for all mankind fulfilled the promise of God to redeem the darkness. "O Little town of Bethlehem, how still we see thee lie! Above thy deep and dreamless sleep the silent stars go by. Yet in thy dark streets shineth the everlasting Light. The hopes and fears of all the years are met in Thee tonight."

One of my favorite verses, that has been used on occasion, is Eph. 5: 11, 13, "And do not participate in the unfruitful deeds of darkness, but instead expose them…But all things become visible when they are exposed by the light." Not only are we given light, but we are to take the light and not be afraid to expose the darkness around us and in us. Psalm 27 echoes this thought, "The Lord is my light and my salvation, whom shall I fear? The Lord is the defense of my life, whom shall I dread?" When we risk position and privilege in our culture by being lights, reflecting the Father of Lights (James 1: 17), we have the reassurance that it's part of the purpose for which we were called, "You are the light of the world. A city set on a hill cannot be hidden… Let your light shine before men in such a way that they may see your good works and glorify your Father who is in heaven" (Matt. 5: 14, 16). It's still about love reaching out, taking risks, giving hope and a promise kept.

How long will you stumble along with eyes closed, bumping into things and asking, "Is this it? Will this provide meaning, understanding?" Is Jesus showing another way? Calling, "Come over here!" What is keeping you from the steady glow? What fears are hiding from His floodlight?

Read John 3: 19-21, John 8: 12, John 9: 4-5

What did you notice the second time you read this passage that you didn't the first time?

What part of the real-life example spoke to you?

What thoughts and feelings came to mind?

How is this related to something you've walked through? Or are currently walking with?

Days Three and Four: Truth Dig --facts and lessons

I Am the Light of the World

John 3: 19-21, John 8: 12, John 9: 4-5

As we walk through this life, it's hard not to focus on the darkness, meaning "death" in the form of destruction, deception, and despair. If Jesus is the Light of the World, why is there so much darkness in our world? These passages will give us insight into darkness and light and how to live in the light. Jesus is the Light for dark times.

John 3: 19 – 21 The darkness of men

1. Why do men love the darkness? Use Ephesians 5: 7-15 to help you with your answer.

2. What happens when people come to the light?

3.   What happens when the deeds of men are exposed?

4.   Does the Word seem to indicate that you need to practice the truth, then you can come to the light? Why or Why not?

John 8 12-13 I Am the Light

1.   The Feast of Tabernacles was happening at this time. There were large candelabras in the treasury that projected light throughout Jerusalem. This was an indication of the Glory that showed the way at night for the children of Israel when they were in the wilderness. What is Jesus proclaiming when He says, "I am the Light?"

2.   What offer is He making here in this passage?

John 9: 4-5 The blind man

1.   We so often see the physical healing – do you think there was a spiritual healing? Why or Why not?

2. What is the key spiritual truth you see in this passage (washing and seeing)?

What does this mean to me? Why do we have darkness in *our* lives?

When we know Jesus, should that keep all the darkness out of our lives?

How does Psalm 119: 105 and Matthew 25: 1-8 apply to this passage?

Ask God to show you the darkness in your own life, then confess those things to Him. Let Him shine His light in those very places, as you release the grip of those things fully. Praise Him for being your light in a very dark world, and willingly let Him illuminate your path each day.

Day Five: Now What...?

What promise, desire, warning, command, or word of encouragement are you to pay attention to?

What action will you take --today? (Even if it's to "wait"). Record what you did about it.

-- and how God is working.

What do you need from Him?

Life Response -- Briefly explain why these verses are important to you? Try phrasing your answer in "I Am" statements (like the prayer on Day One) by recording your need and how The Light of the World can meet that need, regardless of your doubts. Acknowledge these doubts and replace them with the points of truth you just learned. Meditate on this, your personal prayer to God. Use it whenever the need arises to remind yourself of what you're learning through experience and trust, regardless of the size of the trial.

Write your prayer out, sign and date it. Let it be a covenant between your Lord and you.

Chapter Five

Good Shepherd

Read John 10: 11-16

My Good Shepherd

John 10: 11-16, 27-29

Loving Husbandman, faithful Defender.

No sacrifice is too great for You to make on my behalf.

Call to me when I stray

and come after me when I can't find You.

Carry me when I'm hobbled,

but want to follow You.

Show me how to know the difference between a careless hireling

and My own true Shepherd.

Let me enjoy the benefits You desire for me, every day,

safe in Your care.

Day One: Ground Work

Record your initial observations and impressions of both the visual and the prayer:

How are they related to the Scripture reading?

How are these elements preparing your heart to hear God's message to you? (What need are you aware of?)

Day Two: Faith Walk

The Good Shepherd-

After the Light has punched holes in our darkness, the Shepherd longs to walk with us through all our days. It's when we know that He has taken our hand and placed it firmly in His that we'll allow Him to guide us without panic or despair. Entrusting hopes and dreams to the Shepherd, knowing He won't let our feet stumble and hurl us headlong, we let our pace match His. He is like the perfect parent; His Word says, we have a Father who "neither slumbers, nor sleeps" (Ps. 121: 3). He also nurtures us like a mother who, "carries them in Your bosom as a nurse carries a nursing infant..." (Num. 11: 12).

It was in my early days of marriage that I learned some of what was necessary to walk with my Shepherd as a wife, having no human role models I wished to emulate. I was still a college student and trying to finish my program in four years after having attended three schools in that time. The pressure was on as a deadline approached to develop a lesson plan for teaching. My husband had finished his degree a couple of years earlier and was familiar with my assignment, but was not a practicing teacher at the time. He had, instead, started a business and was keeping unpredictable hours, yet promised that he would be home in time to help. The test came in my growth as a wife when he arrived home around bedtime that night and apologized, as I remember, or maybe just made an excuse about some other priority that couldn't wait. Either way, I didn't respond well. The intervening hours ratcheted up my anxiety about the deadline (the next day), and I was not filled with a gracious attitude. I felt hurt, betrayed, abandoned and generally angry with him.

Early into this confrontation, I recall being in a separate room in our tiny apartment and hearing a voice in my head say, "just forgive, as I've forgiven you." Things would have worked out much better if I would have not argued with that suggestion. Feeling justified, I wanted more suffering on my husband's part. But now I know that that was the Shepherd's voice of grace giving us a way out. I forgot that the Shepherd had already lain down His own life; there was nothing more that was required. Forgiveness is possible when one realizes the debt one has been forgiven of oneself. Forgiveness in marriage is an important survival skill if the marriage is to endure. It is a precursor to parenthood forgiveness, another necessary skill in a harmonious home environment. So, after making us both miserable and prolonging a difficult situation, I'm glad at least I could look back and see where I took the detour. We have made mistakes like this since, but not without knowing that the Shepherd is present to help.

The lesson that should have made all the difference is remembering who I'm supposed to trust. Is it human good intentions or divine plans, no matter what the anticipated result. If I have a clear channel of love to and from my Shepherd, without the interference of self-centered lies and superior attitudes, I can weather disappointments much better. There is a wonderful image of a trusting child resting in the parent's care expressed in Psalm 132: 2, "Surely I have composed and quieted my soul; like a weaned child rests against his mother, my soul is… within me."

Is it time yet to yield to One who loves you enough to lead you? Have you listened to the wrong voices, only to have all hope dashed again and again? Do you even believe that such a One exists? That His voice can be believed, trusted?

Read John 10: 11-16

What did you notice the second time you read this passage that you didn't the first time?

What part of the real-life example spoke to you?

What thoughts and feelings came to mind?

How is this related to something you've walked through? Or are currently walking with?

Days Three and Four:
Truth Dig --facts and lessons

I am the Good Shepherd

John 10: 11-16

Jesus is called the Lamb of God. How can He be
the Lamb of God and at the same time be the Good
Shepherd? This may sound like mixed metaphors
but is one of the greatest truths in Scripture. He has
come down and identified himself with us who are the
sheep – but He is the Shepherd also. The fact that He
is the Good Shepherd emphasizes the deity of Christ.

John 10: 11-13 The Good Shepherd

   1. How does Jesus define the Good Shepherd in
      verse 11 of this passage?

   2. In Hebrews 13: 20 Jesus is identified as the
      Great Shepherd of the sheep. What does the
      term mean?

3. In 1 Peter 5:4 Jesus is identifies as the Chief
    Shepherd. What does that mean?

4. Put this all together. When we say Jesus is the
    Shepherd we should think of what?

5. In John 10:12 there is a person described as a
    hireling. Who is the hireling? Who could the
    hireling be today?

John 10: 14-15 Knowing Jesus

1. How does Jesus know us?

2. How do we know Jesus (Philippians 3:10, Matt. 16:13-17)?

3. In this connection we should read what God says about shepherds in His message through Ezekiel in Chapter 34. What does it say about knowing Jesus?

4. Why is it important to know Jesus? List several reasons (see also Ps. 23).

John 10: 16, Isaiah 56: 8 A flock

1. What does one flock mean? Who is going to be in the flock?

What does this mean to me? What are the duties of a Good Shepherd? In a few words explain why these verses are important to you?

Check these Scriptures: 1 Samuel 17: 34-36, Genesis 29: 2-10, Jeremiah 33: 12-13, 1 Chronicles 4: 39-41, Luke 15: 4-5, Isaiah 40:11, Matthew 9: 36.

Praise The Good Shepherd for all He does and is.

What is He calling you to do in response?

Day Five: Now What...?

What promise, desire, warning, command, or word of encouragement are you to pay attention to?

What action will you take --today? (Even if it's to "wait"). Record what you did about it.

-- and how God is working.

What do you need from Him?

Life Response -- Briefly explain why these verses
are important to you? Try phrasing your answer in
"I Am" statements (like the prayer on Day One) by
recording your need and how The Good Shepherd
can meet that need, regardless of your doubts.
Acknowledge these doubts and replace them with
the points of truth you just learned. Meditate on this,
your personal prayer to God. Use it whenever the
need arises to remind yourself of what you're learning
through experience and trust, regardless of the size of
the trial.

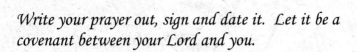

Write your prayer out, sign and date it. Let it be a covenant between your Lord and you.

Chapter Six

The Door

Read John 10: 1-10

I Am the Door

Jesus, the Door

John 10: 7-9 (see also Rev. 3:5, 20)

In a world of falseness, danger, and want,

You are the only entrance into abundance.

Real life begins with a response to the invitation,

 "Enter in."

Let me find true pasture

as I freely accept all You've prepared

in pleasant places, safe in sight of the sheepfold,

where rest and refreshment are possible.

Everywhere else can't sustain my spirit

or satisfy my unfailing needs.

Door II

Entrance into unimagined grace, threshold over which I am called to cross.

Divine life laid down to pay my way out of a world of thieves and robbers.

My true Shepherd is the Door, and His Spirit guards the entrance of the beloved.

I hear my name, and I go forth after Him who summons me.

Stunning green pastures, lovely still waters because of His presence walking close to me.

As I pass through the door, He carefully examines every part of me, to rid me of harmful effects of contact with life outside.

He searches patiently, and prepares me to be comforted in the sheepfold, away from predators who try to steal or destroy the sheep.

I'm home, safe inside, again.

Day One: Ground Work

Record your initial observations and impressions of
both the visual and the prayer:

How are they related to the Scripture reading?

How are these elements preparing your heart to hear
God's message to you? (What need are you aware of?)

Day Two: Faith Walk

The Door-

My husband and I were having a pleasant summer evening at home when we received the call from the hospital chaplain. I had muted the old movie we were watching so that he could hear the speaker on the other end. "Yes, my name is Weikel," I heard my husband say, " and my son's name is Chad... Yes, that's right... what is this about?" My heart started to race. Within minutes we were headed to the emergency room with no more information, but that our son had been a passenger in a serious accident, and we would know more when we got there. Because the last couple of years had been an intense season of trials and loss for us, we responded by praying to a familiar source, a powerful, wise, loving heavenly Father. "Lord God, please protect our son... be merciful... Your will be done."

The details are not important, except to say that our son's liver was lacerated and several ribs had been broken. The driver had hit a tree at a high rate of speed, and the impact was on the passenger's side. The surgeon on call had said that they had done what they could, and the next 24-72 hours would tell the story. "For your son to survive, we had to put him in a medically-induced coma to keep him from moving, in order to give the liver a chance and keep the ribs from doing further damage to the lungs. We will move him into the ICU soon," he said.

After my husband and I moved to the ICU waiting room, it occurred to us to make some phone calls for prayer support from friends. All we could manage were a few calls and gave more names and numbers to them to complete. Because this was a hospital associated with a religious community, we noticed some paintings on the walls with

Scripture. One near our waiting area quoted Is. 41: 10-
11, "Do not fear, for I am with you; do not anxiously
look about you, for I am your God. I will strengthen
you, surely I will help. Surely I will uphold you with My
righteous right hand." My husband stayed that night at the
hospital, repeating those words over our son throughout
the night. We boldly came before the Throne of our God
with our petitions and claimed His sole possession of our
son. This part of the journey was to take nearly four weeks
in the hospital, with additional procedures and surgeries.
It was apparent, however, that for my husband and I, we
had a choice. We chose to walk through the Door to faith
in our Lord, no matter where this might lead. Jesus is the
Door and we belong to Him. Our Lord supplied comfort,
strength, faith, wisdom, the body of Christ, and focus
during a chaotic time.

We believe this wasn't a random event, but one that fit into
a master plan to refine and shape those touched by it. Is
there a Door of opportunity for you? Or maybe a Door
man has closed with access denied? Through the hurt
and frustration, the fear and longing, is there a better way?
Can you get past the anger and paralysis to find what only
God can give?

Read John 10: 1-10

What did you notice the second time you read this passage that you didn't the first time?

What part of the real-life example spoke to you?

What thoughts and feelings came to mind?

How is this related to something you've walked through? Or are currently walking with?

Days Three and Four:
Truth Dig —facts and lessons

I Am the Door of the Sheep

John 10: 1-10

The ancient sheepfold of that day still exists in many towns today. It was a public sheepfold. In the evening all the shepherds who lived in the town would bring their sheep into the sheepfold and turn them in for the night. They would entrust them to the doorkeeper who kept the sheep; then they would go home for the night. The next morning the shepherds would identify themselves to the doorkeeper, and he would let them in the door to get their sheep.

John 10: 1-2 Door into the sheepfold

1. What claim is Jesus making here?

2. What prophecies in the Old Testament is Jesus fulfilling (Galatians 4: 4, Luke 1: 32, Micah 5: 2, Isaiah 7: 14, Isaiah 11: 1)?

3. What was meant by a thief and a robber?

John 10: 3 Jesus calls

1. Who is the doorkeeper?(see also Rev. 3:7-8)

2. Jesus calls his sheep by name. Can you think of any people in the New Testament that Jesus called? Who? How did each respond? (Matt. 10, Acts 26, John 20:1-18)

3. When Jesus returns, will we hear our own name? (Phil. 4:3, I Thess. 4:16, Rev.2: 17, 20:15, 22:17)

4. When Jesus leads them out of the sheepfold what does that represent?

John 10: 6-10 The Door

1. When Jesus uses this term "the door" what is He referring to here in this passage?

2. How do we have abundant life through Jesus?

3. Why doesn't the sheep hear the voice of the thief and robber?

4. How do you enter through Jesus?

What does this mean to me? Place yourself in the sheepfold. Jesus calls you out of the sheepfold. What belongs to you now?

Tell God in what "the door" means to you, giving you access to all of who He is, remembering that there is no other way to gain access.

Day Five: Now What...?

What promise, desire, warning, command, or word of encouragement are you to pay attention to?

What action will you take --today? (Even if it's to "wait"). Record what you did about it.

-- and how God is working.

What do you need from Him?

Life Response -- Briefly explain why these verses
are important to you? Try phrasing your answer in
"I Am" statements (like the prayer on Day One) by
recording your need and how The Door can meet that
need, regardless of your doubts. Acknowledge these
doubts and replace them with the points of truth you
just learned. Meditate on this, your personal prayer
to God. Use it whenever the need arises to remind
yourself of what you're learning through experience
and trust, regardless of the size of the trial.

Write your prayer out, sign and date it. Let it be a covenant between your Lord and you.

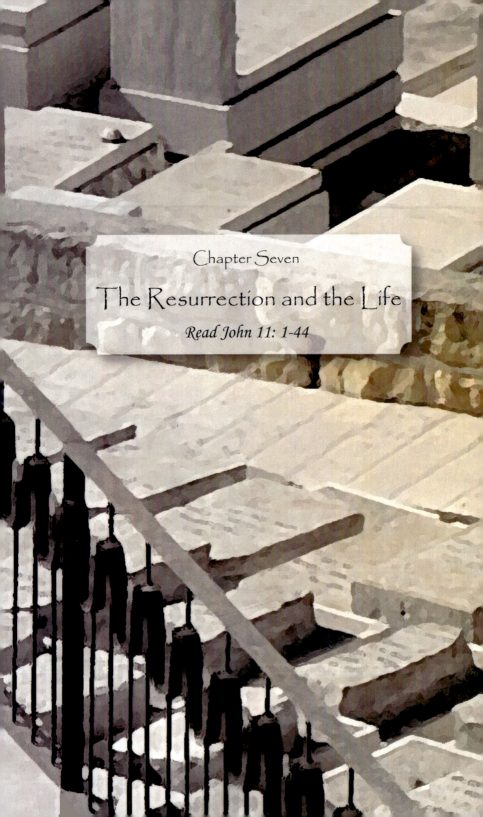

Chapter Seven

The Resurrection and the Life

Read John 11: 1-44

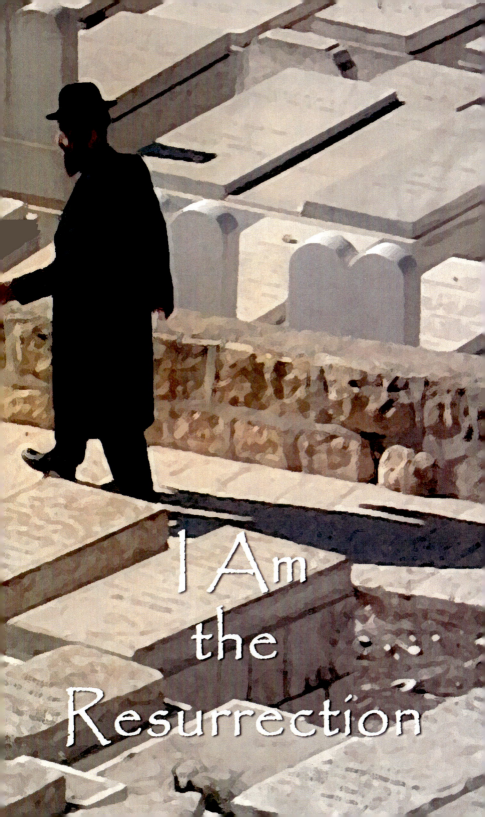

I Am
the
Resurrection

...and the Life

Jesus, the Resurrection and the Life
John 11:25-26

Death happens when we don't expect it,

Oftentimes.

It's hard to prepare for it.

Mary & Martha, shocked when Lazarus died,

accused You of not caring enough, not being on time.

Equally grieved, You demonstrated Your sorrow,

like a true friend, family.

By Your power and love, show me the Father's glory.

Perfect me by demonstrating the same promise today.

Roll away the stone, remove the stench of death,

Be my Life, my Resurrection,

for those behind the veil live because of You.

Our inheritance is Your kingdom now and forever,
at the last breath,

beyond the earth's atmosphere.

May I believe it, until my last sigh.

Resurrection and Life II

Supernatural gift, life with You and in You.

Worthy of worship, blessed name above all names.

No lasting sorrow of death, odd mixture of unutterable joy and grief,

flowing into the brain and out of the heart,

straining to believe, to rest.

Peeking, glimpses of eternal realities, not yet understood.

Knowing supreme loss, yet abundant grace.

Death, families witnessing a miracle birthed of sacrifice and love.

Walking on a different plane, in faith, holding on, being held onto.

Praise in the pain; unique privilege not sought.

You've been here before, you tell me. I've read all about it over and over.

Now I see, in a new way, the journey and the awesome Power,

perfected in dramatic circumstances.

*My head knows the words of truth, and my heart is
wanting to understand.*

*I fall at your feet, like Mary, and see your eyes
filling with tears, too.*

*Called forth! Ian, LaVerne, Morrie, Bill ... running
into Your arms, only to be*

rocked and soothed.

*Love rescuing, not perishing. Glory yet to be
revealed.*

Miracle of faith; Your way is right.

*Put down the useless trappings of this life: uniform,
housedress, hospital gown.*

Unbind the grave clothes on my heart.

Resurrect me to new life, too.

*Stand me on the Rock, as solid as the rock that
covered the tomb,*

assured, foundational.

*Cover me beneath the shade of the Rock, and drape
your protection*

over and around me, secure,

no longer tormented.

Hide me from the storm,

surging, flooding, constant rain;

Yet take me through it, through the parched land, winds wild about me.

Let me not just see the rock of a headstone, but an altar,

memorial to Your goodness and faithfulness.

Promise fulfilled; new life, new name that only You know,

written on a white stone.

Each one entering the glorious Kingdom.

But Your house, the Spirit that lives in me, motioning me, directing my steps,

keeping me from falling flat, never to get up,

Saying, "What seems to be is not what is."

Job confessed, "…But He knows the way I take.

When He has tried me, I shall come forth as gold…

I have treasured the Words of His mouth more than necessary food."

Jesus, Your power, when You finished Your race,

split the rocks, tore the veil, shook the earth,

until the very tombs were opened.

You, Son of God, left no room for doubt.

The gates of hell will not overpower Your work.

In God's name,

we all drink from the same Rock which follows us,

goes before us,

over countless generations.

Reconciliation to You. Redemption is all that
matters.

Let me bring Your light

to give sight to those who have lost their way

and want to find it again.

Glorify Your name; show me

where,

how.

Day One: Ground Work

Record your initial observations and impressions of
both the visual and the prayer:

How are they related to the Scripture reading?

How are these elements preparing your heart to hear
God's message to you? (What need are you aware of?)

Day Two: Faith Walk

The Resurrection and the Life-

A little over two years previous to our younger son's
accident and subsequent recovery, we were part of another
miracle of God. Chad's resurrection is in process, but our
older son, Ian, has been resurrected to his heavenly home.
In the spring, just two days after Easter, Ian's humvee was
hit by an IED. Capt. Ian Weikel was doing his command
in Iraq, his second deployment in the war, on that day like
so many others. We received the news while visiting our
daughter-in-law and grandson near Ft. Hood in Texas.

My husband and our daughter-in-law were doing yard
work when the two men in dress greens appeared suddenly
from behind our RV parked at the curb. I was in the
kitchen making dinner and babysitting when I heard
our daughter-in-law say in a strange voice, "Beth, get
Jonathan!" Together we gathered in the living room to
listen to that telegram as though through a fog. Just a few
sentences to say that Ian was gone from us. The army has
procedures in place when this event happens, so shortly
after the chaplain and that young soldier left, a team of
individuals came to offer assistance.

All l can remember is that I wanted these strangers to
leave and take all the noise with them. After making
plane reservations for my husband to fly home to tell his
father and our other son, they did. But then something
remarkable happened. Another team of people came to
the house. Ian and daughter-in-law attended a warm,
Bible-teaching church in the next town. Their pastor, his
wife, and several elder couples walked into our lives at
that dark moment. One man we had met as Ian's Sunday
school teacher searched the room for us upon entering and

immediately took our hands in his and asked, "Do you believe Jesus is alive?"

"Yes," we both said.

"Then your son, Ian, is alive!" he proclaimed. He locked eyes with us and repeated this drill to us over and over, and added, "There will come a time when you will doubt this, but remember, Jesus Christ is risen and so is your son."

Those words lodged in our souls. I have since recalled earlier on the same day as I was reading a book called, *Waking the Dead*, that it spoke on the same theme. It impressed me then with the thought that I should have already understood, but really didn't in the way I did as I read it, "The Good News is not Jesus on the cross; it's the resurrection… The disciples weren't persecuted and martyred because they told about the historic event of the cross. No, the controversy that they gave their lives to was the belief that Jesus was resurrected." All hope rests on this miraculous fact. God's plan was to redeem mankind with the resurrection, not just the cross. Because our sins are paid for, we have a home with this same Jesus, forever with our Lord.

Where are your dead areas, or what have you given up on? Do believe that Jesus can offer renewed hope to any one of these lost causes?

What is there to lose? Can you use Someone with the power over death—in any form? The Good News is not just the cross; it's the resurrection!

Read John 11: 1-44

What did you notice the second time you read this passage that you didn't the first time?

What part of the real-life example spoke to you?

What thoughts and feelings came to mind?

How is this related to something you've walked through? Or are currently walking with?

Days Three and Four: Truth Dig --facts and lessons

I Am the Resurrection and the Life

John 11: 1-44

Now the supreme question is this: Can Jesus raise the dead? The big question in religion concerns death. Death is a great mystery, but life is practically meaningless if there is no resurrection of the dead. The question to ask any religion is whether it has power over death.

John 11: 1-10 Walking in the day and night

1. When Mary anointed Jesus (John 12), she was doing this for what purpose?

2. The sisters, Mary and Martha, sent word to Jesus of the problem and did not make a request. What implications does this have for our prayers? (see also Luke 7:1-10)

3. What could happen to Jesus if He goes to Judea again?

4. In verse 9 and 10 Jesus is talking about walking in the day and walking in the night. What does this mean? (see also John 12:31-36)

John 11: 11-26 The Resurrection and the Life

1. Why are people afraid of death?

2. Why would the disciples believe if they see the miracle?

3. What was Thomas saying in this passage?

4. Is there something underlying Martha's statement to Jesus (verses 21-22)?

5. What is Jesus saying here when He states that He is the Resurrection and the Life (verses 25-56)?

6. What does Martha believe?

John 11: 27-46 The empathy of Jesus

1. Notice how Mary's response was different
   from her sister's even though her words were
   the same. (Describe this using verses 32-33).

2. Why did Jesus cry?

3. It seems that even people who know of Jesus
   react with doubt and accusation when faced
   with bad news. Where in these passages do
   you see this? Do they think Jesus didn't care?
   (see verse 38)

4. Why did Jesus raise Lazarus? How did
   He involve those who wondered about His
   motives or power? How did He give the
   Father glory?

What does this mean to me? We cannot ignore this miracle and Jesus' statement concerning being the Resurrection and the Life. By what means did Jesus accomplish this?

What kinds of methods did you notice? (see verses 39, 41-44)

What two responses usually accompany the undeniable work of God? (see verses 45, 47-48)

What is your response?

Tell God what you believe.

Then ask Him how to share this truth with others?

Day Five: Now What...?

What promise, desire, warning, command, or word of encouragement are you to pay attention to?

What action will you take --today? (Even if it's to "wait"). Record what you did about it.

-- and how God is working.

What do you need from Him?

Life Response -- Briefly explain why these verses
are important to you? Try phrasing your answer in
"I Am" statements (like the prayer on Day One) by
recording your need and how The Resurrection and
Life can meet that need, regardless of your doubts.
Acknowledge these doubts and replace them with
the points of truth you just learned. Meditate on this,
your personal prayer to God. Use it whenever the
need arises to remind yourself of what you're learning
through experience and trust, regardless of the size of
the trial.

Write your prayer out, sign and date it. Let it be a covenant between your Lord and you.

Chapter Eight

The Way, the Truth, and the Life

Read John 14: 1-6

I Am the Way, the Truth, the Life

Jesus, the Way, the Truth, and the Life

John 14: 6

Great I Am, healer of my heart, take my hand in Yours and lead me in the everlasting way.

Keep my weary feet from stumbling off the path, into doubt and despair.

Truth-teller, in whom is no guile, or deceit, speak Your Word into my very soul, seal it for all time, only to produce wisdom and faith.

Let fears flee, as Your true character shines its light into the deepest recesses of my dark, troubled mind.

Your will, Your way, lived out in places You've planned from the beginning, by means of Your Spirit

"Love God and love one another, proving to be My disciples… follow Me… and I will come again to receive you to Myself,"

Burn this longing into my daily experience.

Show me the Father, as I follow the Son. Let me not miss any steps.

This Way,

This Truth,

This Life.

Way, Truth, Life II

Only source of meaning,

holy, yet compassionate;

mighty, yet tender.

Lead me past the carnage of false promises clutched

and dashed dreams entertained.

Open my eyes to see clearly, and my heart to desire fully

*to follow the narrow way that leads to eternal
dwelling places,*

personally prepared by My Creator and Lord,

now and forever.

*Liberate me—deep within my soul—to believe all
that You say.*

Glorify Yourself in me by Your grace.

By Your will, rebirth my will to become Your child,

growing ever more into Your likeness.

Grant, by Your favor, the miracle of knowing You,

loving You more than the things of this life.

Forgive my many missteps and wanderings.

Draw me ever closer to Your side

to share the life offered by Your visitation for me.

Day One: Ground Work

Record your initial observations and impressions of both the visual and the prayer:

How are they related to the Scripture reading?

How are these elements preparing your heart to hear God's message to you? (What need are you aware of?)

Day Two: Faith Walk

The Way, the Truth, and the Life-

Do you remember the first time you were betrayed? Was there a time you remember feeling empathy for someone else and an unkindness done to them? Can you recall when you realized that not everyone could be trusted? How did you respond? How did that fact or event change you? I dare say that most of us became guarded, frightened, less vulnerable, less free to be ourselves.

Living in a home where my parents didn't know how to love each other, I saw this at an early age, before school age, in fact. My eyes were open, as well as those of my slightly older brother, to the reality that life would not be easy in the world of adults. There were situations and complications that we lived with that we were not prepared to understand, let alone protect ourselves against. If it had not been for God's clear intervention and presence, I would have gone the way of many young people today, finding solace, meaning, escape in any number of destructive ways.

As a young child, I heard God's call and gave my life to Him. Nothing much changed in my day to day experience, but I had the assurance that Someone larger than any human cared about me and that I belonged to Him. So, as I grew in things of the Lord, my spirit resonated with teaching such as, II Peter 1: 2-4 , "Grace and peace be yours in abundance through the[head and heart] knowledge of God and of Jesus our Lord. His divine power has given us everything we need for life and godliness... Who has called us by His own glory and goodness. Through these He has given us His very great and precious promises..." I was hearing that I had all that I needed to live successfully in this life, no matter the circumstances or who had authority over me. As I got to know God personally and intimately, because of the Spirit that He gave me, I would be participating in the life He wanted me to have, not life by default.

There was hope after all. His reassuring Word was everywhere, "My soul waits in silence for God only; from Him is my salvation. He only is my Rock... my stronghold; I shall not be greatly shaken" (Ps. 62: 2). I also learned that I had an advocate, Someone who stuck up for me, "...He [Jesus] is able to save forever those who draw near to God through Him and always lives to make intercession for them" (Heb. 7: 25). It wasn't up to me or anyone else to take care of me and make sure I knew what to do, "I am confident of this: that the One who has begun a good work in you will go on developing it until the day of Jesus Christ [His return]" (Phil. 1: 6, Phil. Trans.).

And when I read about the people mentioned in the Bible and some of the hardships they faced, I saw how their lives were directed and changed when they believed God. "Is anything too difficult for the Lord? At the appointed time I will return to you... and Sarah shall have a son" (Gen. 18: 14). There were so many examples of everyday individuals who walked with God, or who God chose for His own reasons, who saw His wonders and knew He was in control of events that touched their lives—Mary, Daniel, Ruth, Elijah, Joshua, Gideon, Esther.

Anything that I've achieved and any trial that I've dealt with, I know Who has been there accompanying me every step. Amid the doubts and frustration, the adulation and rejoicing, He shares every part and will until I go home to Him. His truth can be trusted. To follow Jesus is to find our way. Living life in His presence and leaning on

His wisdom and power is the opposite of futility. King
Solomon, who had everything he could possibly want and
lived to regret it, concluded that real life is finding purpose
in God's plans. "And follow the impulses of your heart
and the desires of your eyes. Yet know that God will bring
you to judgment for all these things. So remove vexation
from your heart and put away pain from your body, because
childhood and the prime of life are fleeting. Remember
your Creator in the days of your youth, before the evil days
come and the years draw near when you will say, 'I have no
delight in them'" (Eccl. 11: 9-10, 12: 1). No longer having
to beat the air and strive against all odds is what Jesus
came to give. The other choice is "Vanity of vanities, all is
vanity... all things are wearisome" (Eccl. 1: 2, 8).

The Way, the Truth, the Life, quite the package. Even
if only one of these were real, what a remarkable claim.
Someone who actually knows the way or tells the truth—
always, and gives life, not takes from us. Someone who
freely offers all that we need and really want. In the
current vernacular, this is Jesus' mission statement. He
completed His work on our behalf so that each of us would
no longer be afraid or have to fake it. His life in exchange
for our limitations now and forever... His goodness, His
mercy, His peace, any questions?

Read John 14: 1-6

What did you notice the second time you read this passage that you didn't the first time?

What part of the real-life example spoke to you?

What thoughts and feelings came to mind?

How is this related to something you've walked through? Or are currently walking with?

Days Three and Four: Truth Dig --facts and lessons

I am the Way, and the Truth, and the Life

John 14: 1-6

Peter has just declared they He would lay down his life for Jesus. Then Jesus said that Peter would deny Him three times (13:37-38). In this next chapter the Lord is still speaking to Peter, in order to bring Peter through the darkness of denial and back into a right relationship with God. This chapter cushions the shock of sin and denial that we all have experienced. Jesus comforts us in our deepest needs.

John 14: 1-2 Comfort and peace

1. People throughout the world are seeking comfort and peace. When is your "heart troubled?"

2. What does Jesus say is the basis of comfort and peace?

3. What is Jesus saying when He says, "believe in God, believe also in Me"?

4. Why does it produce comfort knowing that Jesus is preparing a place for us?

5. The word for "mansion" means dwelling place. What does this mean for us?

John 14: 3-5 Promises

1. In verse 3 there are some promises Jesus makes to believers. What are these promises, and how does each reassure you?

2. Jesus' words convey that He is sure that His disciples understand where He is going. What would startle the disciples when Jesus makes this statement in verse 3 and 4?

3. What is Jesus trying to teach his disciples when He refers to preparing a place?

4. Thomas asks such a wonderful question. Why is it important to ask? Do you have the same question?

John 14: 6 Way, Truth, Life

1. Study verses 7-29 before responding to the claim
Jesus makes when He declares to His disciples that
He is the Way, the Truth, and the Life. What does He
mean? Find Scripture to support your answers.

    a. The Way:

    b. The Truth:

    c. The Life:

What does this mean to me? These verses have a strong impact in our lives. What is God showing you in each of these areas?

How does He want you to respond to Him?

Praise the Father, Son, and Holy Spirit for the gift each is to you.

Confess your need for each and your dependence on and submission to this reality.

Day Five: Now What...?

What promise, desire, warning, command, or word of encouragement are you to pay attention to?

What action will you take --today? (Even if it's to "wait"). Record what you did about it.

-- and how God is working.

What do you need from Him?

Life Response -- Briefly explain why these verses are important to you? Try phrasing your answer in "I Am" statements (like the prayer on Day One) by recording your need and how The Way, the Truth, and the Life can meet that need, regardless of your doubts. Acknowledge these doubts and replace them with the points of truth you just learned. Meditate on this, your personal prayer to God. Use it whenever the need arises to remind yourself of what you're learning through experience and trust, regardless of the size of the trial.

Write your prayer out, sign and date it. Let it be a covenant between your Lord and you.

Chapter Nine

The True Vine

Read John 15: 1-14

I Am
the Vine

Jesus, the True Vine

John 15

I am Yours and You are mine; abide.

Plant this life root, in the rich soil of Your grace
and nurture my days with the sunshine and rain of
Your presence,
until the shoots appear, promising fruitful, tender
buds of holiness.

Wise Vinedresser, carefully and thoroughly clear out
the deadness,
lift up errant stems, and tie them securely to train them.

Prune and shape fruitful, healthy branches severely,
only to create desired strength and purpose.

Life and meaning exist in the Vine, joy to the full.

Apply Your patient skill and abundant mercy in the
process.

I lay my life in Your hands, to become the sweetness,
the lasting fragrance of Your glory.

Chosen to abide, then crushed to release the bounty
of the work,
the Love poured in, Father and Son.

"Taste and see that the Lord is good."

Jesus, the True Vine II

"*Abide in me*
and I in you."
Life source, drawing forth only from the Vine,
sustaining vitality at times,
others times, just a stump.
Pruning that allows richer, more abundant fruit,
severe, thorough, necessary.
Your Word, life itself,
may it feed me so that life buds,
bringing glorious blossoms, showy, luscious,
undeniable fruit.
Christ, the Vine, His church the branches,
Love poured out in all directions,
feeding joy to the full.
Abide, stay connected--
For meaning, in hopeful goodness, mercy.
In training, being lifted again and again by unseen
hands, carefully.
Wisely the plan continues season after season.
Getting stronger, more vital,
Sending fresh shoots, nourished in ancient root.
Patient progress, persistent process.
Chosen, attended to,
growing on steep hillsides,
ever reaching to the sun.

Vine III

Jesus, mighty, ancient vine,
wrap Yourself around me--
with Your sure and steady sustenance.
Your abiding Word and constant presence
produce joy that drips down,
sending healing to my pruned places,
ugly stumps of self-will and meager efforts.
Nurture my tender shoots of budding new life.
Train my parts to climb and grow,
as I am supported among untold neighboring
branches,
attended by the Vinedresser—loving, experienced.
Let me enjoy the fruit of Your labors,
season after season.
My all-sufficient Source,
help me understand the necessary cycles of
fruitfulness—
thorough pruning, dormancy, awakening to new life,
beautiful fresh buds, and full flowering,
thriving in the light and warmth of daily sun and
refreshing rain.
Fruit grown on steep slopes, ripe for harvest.

Day One: Ground Work

Record your initial observations and impressions of both the visual and the prayer:

How are they related to the Scripture reading?

How are these elements preparing your heart to hear God's message to you? (What need are you aware of?)

Day Two: Faith Walk

The True Vine-

Because of the richness of the preceding claims of Jesus,
it hardly seems necessary to want more: living water that
refreshes and cleanses, bread that sustains and satisfies,
light to dispel the darkness, a good shepherd who leads,
corrects, calls to us, a door to pasture and protection,
resurrection that brings life from death, the way, the truth,
the life, in a world that's lost these concepts to a relativistic
reality. But Jesus and the Father, along with the indwelling
of the Holy Spirit, want even more for those who put their
hope in Them. This final claim is so important to all the
others, because the implied response to it is "to remain."

While studying this section of the Gospel of John recently
with a group of women who had been meeting over time
to explore a deeper level of discipleship, we wrestled
with the words and their meanings, as to what God's
job was and what was required of us. There seemed to
be a clear division of responsibility. The concept that
emerged repeatedly for us was "to remain." In a world
that shows lack of commitment in so many arenas, this
simple statement was inescapable. Where were the
models? Fragmentation and detachment are the order of
the day. Family life is being redefined to include yours,
mine, and ours until we get bored and find something
more appealing; business practices allow for short-term
association as needs change; and the thirty-year mortgage
is rarely necessary, since households move on the average
of every six years. Among the younger generation,
disposable consumerism is the norm; no one expects to
keep and fix an appliance or electronic device, just replace
it with the state-of-the art model.

Press the "easy button," the advertisers say. What an
illusion. There is nothing easy about maturing, ripening,
or becoming something of real value. To keep this analogy
of the vineyard, how special is this year's vintage? Or
how long does it take to produce anything in nature
that is desirable? Oil, diamonds, forests? Apart from
modern society, it would seem to indicate that a process
is involved. While going through a time of molding,
myself, I heard the call from Scripture, "Let's go down to
the potter's house" (Jer. 18). The prophet Jeremiah was a
courageous individual, though sometimes reluctantly, who
was on intimate terms with the living God and was used by
Him to bring God's message to a rebellious nation, God's
own possession. Jeremiah often was taught by God by
becoming the visual aid to the children of Israel. On this
occasion, God used a common practice of making clay
pots, utilitarian objects of everyday life.

Those of us who have dabbled in ceramics classes know
a little about the art and difficulties involved in making
a simple clay pot that's useful. To produce something of
beauty and function, the artist must manage two important
elements, water and pressure. The water helps the potter
as much as the vessel: not enough water and the clay can't
be shaped in the hands of the potter, too much water and
the vessel becomes weak. Pressure skillfully applied
is necessary as well: to keep the vessel centered on the
wheel and not become deformed and to form the desired
design for an intended purpose. It takes months and years
to become adept and knowledgeable as a potter. He has
to have foresight and see the object he wants to make. In
other words, he must know ahead of time the outcome and
recognize when his work is finished.

Jeremiah allowed God to give him insight into this process
and hear its message. A prophet often gives a warning and

this time was no different. God declared Himself to be the Potter, with all the authority over the pot that that implies. All He required of the nation of Israel was that they turn back from their independent (and evil) ways. They refused "to remain" as they were instructed. "'For we are going to follow our own plans, and each of us will act according to the stubbornness of his evil heart'" (Jer. 18: 12). Now they faced calamity. The consequence God allowed was to let them experience the full impact of their decision. "'For my people have forgotten Me... Like the east wind I will scatter them before the enemy; I will show them My back and not My face...'" (Jer. 18: 15, 17). So when Jeremiah took God's message to them, they responded by wanting to harm him rather than taking the opportunity offered them to turn to God and avoid His wrath. People haven't changed much.

So, to appreciate the True Vine, one has to evaluate what one is clinging to. What are you wrapping yourself around? Is it life-producing, worth the effort? What does Jesus promise instead? What's already available, and how does it work?

Read John 15: 1-14

What did you notice the second time you read this passage that you didn't the first time?

What part of the real-life example spoke to you?

What thoughts and feelings came to mind?

How is this related to something you've walked through? Or are currently walking with?

Days Three and Four:
Truth Dig—facts and lessons

I am the True Vine

John 15: 1-14

By using this figure of speech, it is very clear that what's important is not identification with a religion, or a ceremony, or an organization that is essential. We are to be identified with Christ. We are in Christ by the baptism of the Holy Spirit the moment we trust Christ as our Savior and are reborn as a child of God. This Scripture is discussing fruit-bearing after we accept Jesus.

John 15: 1-14

1. What does the word "true" mean in this passage? (Start by looking this word up in the dictionary).

2. When Jesus referred to a vine in verse 1, what did the disciples think of in their Old Testament reference? (Psalm 80: 8-9, Isaiah 5: 1-7, Jeremiah 2: 21)

3. What does the vinedresser mean in this context? (another word used for vinedresser is "gardener")

4. How do you get "in Christ?" What action word of the believer is repeated?

5. In this passage Jesus is also talking about fruit bearing. List these verses.

6. What is fruit (Galatians 5: 22-23)?

How is fruit possible in a life?

How does it last?

7. Where does He take the branch that does not bear fruit?

What does He do to the branch that bears fruit?

8. How can the Word clean you? (see also Matt. 7:24, Mark 4:14-20, John 6:63, Rom. 10:8-10, Col. 3:16, I Tim. 4:1-6, James 1:21, Heb. 4:12)

9. What does it mean to abide in Christ? (some versions use "remain") Look up "abide" in the dictionary.

According to verse 6 what happens to the branch that does not abide?

10. What commandments is Jesus referring to here in this passage?

11. What connection to love is mentioned?

12. Is obedience essential to abiding?

13. How did Jesus and the Father model this?

14. Is there a promise in this passage about prayer?

15. If you do not keep His commandments can you have joy?

Whose joy is it?

What does this mean to me? How do you know if you're bearing fruit?

What fruit do you wish was more evident in your life?

What changes can you make to allow more fruit bearing?

The tendency with verses like these is to assume conditions that don't exist. Whose job is it to produce fruit that lasts?

What is required of the believer?

Acknowledge the Vine and the Vinedresser in your life. Thank each for the work they do as the source of spiritual life and health that affects not only your life, but those around you.

Commit to "abide/remain" in His love and His words. Write this out.

Day Five: Now What...?

What promise, desire, warning, command, or word of encouragement are you to pay attention to?

What action will you take --today? (Even if it's to "wait"). Record what you did about it.

-- and how God is working.

What do you need from Him?

Life Response -- Briefly explain why these verses
are important to you? Try phrasing your answer in
"I Am" statements (like the prayer on Day One) by
recording your need and how The Vine can meet that
need, regardless of your doubts. Acknowledge these
doubts and replace them with the points of truth you
just learned. Meditate on this, your personal prayer
to God. Use it whenever the need arises to remind
yourself of what you're learning through experience
and trust, regardless of the size of the trial.

Write your prayer out, sign and date it. Let it be a covenant between your Lord and you.

Epilogue

This study in the "I Am's" is meant to help you, the reader and disciple, to become aware of your own journey and pay attention to all that Jesus is offering each day, especially in the waiting. One way to do that is to keep a record of His character expressed in the blessings and challenges: His faithfulness, unfailing love, incorruptible nature, truth and wisdom evidenced along the way.

You are a living witness to how Jesus demonstrates His adequacy and love for you. Praise Him with eyes of faith for being more than enough, now and always. You will not be able to contain your worship if you trust in the unseen places, the silence, the suffering, until as Deut. 30: 10-20 declares, "…if you turn to the Lord, your God, with all your heart and soul. For this command is not too difficult for you, nor is it out of reach… But the word is very near you, in your mouth and in your heart, that you may observe it… So choose life… by loving the Lord your God, by obeying His voice, and by holding fast to Him: for this is your life and the length of your days, that you may live in the land…"

Jehovah God called Himself "I Am Who I Am" to Moses in Old Testament times (Ex. 3:14), and Jesus, His one and only Son, reveals God to His disciples in the Gospels. By the indwelling Holy Spirit, the Christ follower today is linked to the same power, love, and presence of the living "I Am." Nothing is diminished; His plan continues through all generations. The question remains, "how will we respond?"

Psalm 78 is a timeless expression of the guidance and strength of the eternal Lord, in Whom belongs all our confidence. It reminds the hearer not to forget His wondrous works or His covenant to His children. It reviews the history of Israel and their rebellious ways as a warning. Despite repeated miracles, they "put God to the test"(v.18). They said, "Can God prepare a table in the wilderness?"(v.19)

What follows is a catalog of God's provision and their corresponding ingratitude: "struck a rock, so that waters gushed out...opened the doors of heaven and rained down manna for them to eat... and they did not believe... and did not trust in His salvation...But He, being compassionate, forgave their iniquity...and often restrained His anger... He remembered that they were but flesh... yet, they did not remember His power...and again and again pained the Holy One of Israel... But He led forth His people like sheep...drove out their adversaries... and led them safely, so that they did not fear."

How is your relationship with this long-suffering God? At what part of the cycle are you? Are there idols in the camp? Are you in captivity? Or, are you enjoying your portion and inheritance, though walking in Jesus' footsteps? This more-than-enough Jesus lives. His way is not easy, but sure. What "I Am" are you crying out for? Will you trust Him and believe what He promises? Or do you expect another way? Let's review:

Deity—the benevolent controller, who creates order and knows no impossibilities (Ps. 78:1-4).

Living Water—cleansing, refreshing, not stagnant, putrid pools, giving health and encouragement amid dryness (Ps. 78:13, 15-16).

Bread—satisfaction, complete provision, dispelling hunger, providing appetite in hollow places (Ps. 78:18-19, 25,29).

Light—illumines the darkness, flooding the world with His steady beam, reflecting glory

Good Shepherd—knows out needs, cares, leads, sacrifices, not a hireling (Ps. 78:14,39-40,52).

Door—lays down His life so we can enter in, one way to pasture (Ps.78:70-72, Ps.79:9).

Resurrection & Life—brings life from death, no devices or tricks (Ps. 78:35-37,42).

Way, Truth, Life—trustworthy, clears the path to follow Him, no deceit, doesn't abandon (Ps. 78:43-51,53).

True Vine—source of vitality, shapes, rids of dead wood, trains, useless places pruned, not neglectful (Ps. 78:54-55,60-64).

Jesus, accept nothing less, no one else, don't put Him off, find a place with Him, abide in the I Am. Give Him the problems, the load, the mess. Rest, trust, believe, hope. Accept the only love that never ends. He is more than enough for anything we experience in this life, with its surprises, blows, disappointments, fears.

Paul urges the Corinthians not to fake it, though. We still have that tendency. "but whenever a man turns to the Lord, the veil is taken away…But we all with unveiled face beholding as in a mirror the glory of the Lord, are being transformed into the same image" (II Cor. 3:16-18). Abiding in the Almighty is a mercy gift from the great I Am. Let Him capture your falseness and replace it with freedom by His Spirit. Release the poor attempts, the good intentions, the self-effort. He is waiting to "BE" all that's needed, not just "DO." Pray one more time acknowledging who He is and what He wants from you. Listen to eternal I Am and lay down any hindrances. Spend time worshiping, confessing, asking, thanking. He is here, now and forever.

Appendix A

"I Am's"

Greek words defined

Deity—only begotten of the Father

Creator—makes things that begin to be

Bread—food, manna, beneficent gift, bestowed liberally

Living Water—in full vigor, having vital power in itself

Light—spiritually pure, of truth, knowledge, exposed to full view

Good Shepherd—takes care of, have control, protects, defends, healing the wounded & sick , finding the lost, saving the trapped, sharing His life to earn trust, loving

Door—passage, opportunity bringing salvation, condition in which to be received into the Kingdom

Resurrection & Life*—raised up; fullness of life essentially and ethically, real, genuine, blessed

Way, Truth, Life*—way of thinking... feeling... deciding, road traveled; in fact, reality, free from pretence... deceit... simulation, certainly

Vine-- Christ infuses divine strength and life into His followers ("sap"), imparts to its branches productiveness ("fruit")

Appendix B

Series of Exchanges

Mine	for	Jesus'
my fallen, limited humanity, selfishness		His indwelling deity and being a new creation
my hunger, emptiness		His daily sustenance (bread)
my drought, desperation		His refreshing, transforming streams (living water)
my darkness, stumbling		His pure light exposing the view, now knowing
my panic, woundedness, lostness		His rescue, healing, guidance, and defense (shepherding)
my dead ends		His invitation to eternity with Him, real opportunity (door)
my death, futility		His fullness, raised to genuine blessing (resurrection & life)
my confusion, deception, striving		His path of certainty, free from performing, living in reality (way, truth, life)
my weakness, inadequate self-sufficiency		His supernatural strength, producing worthwhile, lasting results (vine)

Appendix C

The Altar

The use of altars in Hebrew history plays a significant role in picturing God's relationship with man. Its uses are as follows:

1. A place of remembering God's redemptive work (the first altar recorded used to worship God built by Noah, Gen. 8:20).
2. Making a connection between a holy God and his chosen possession by covenant, as evidenced by burnt offering and incense offering; the first to make atonement for sins and the second as a symbol of acceptable prayer before the throne of God.
3. And finally, Jesus' cross, which, for all time, satisfied the payment for man's sinful state and made a way to reconciliation with his Maker, once and for all. Christ exchanged His own righteousness for our sin. Seems like an unfair trade, but nonetheless, it was God's way, His only plan.

And because this grace has been extended to us, it is now our choice to continue to live lives worthy of this gift. No longer slaves to sin, we lay our lives on the altar, and cooperate with the transforming work made possible in Christ. Since Christ's claims in His "I Am" statements are active in the believer's life and experience, we are compelled to submit past habits and desires to His control. He has made us co-ministers of reconciliation and requires us to surrender to His leadership in our hearts, minds, and actions. This is not always a smooth road, but a necessary one. Walking by faith in the living God and His Word is the way through this fallen world.

A Prayer of Commitment

In each area discussed in this study, find a portion of Scripture to reflect on and purposely release past impulses and inadequate ways of responding to circumstances to God, Who will replace them with Himself in new ways. Follow this pattern each time you are aware of the need to have Him become that "I Am" in your life:

    a. Praise and worship for Who He is in His Word, related to this specific area

    b. Confession, as you agree with Him about this need or blind spot in your life

    c. Ask Him to take this false effort and replace it with His fullness and power

    d. Offer thanks, believing that He will perform the work according to His will

Biography

I've been the mother of two talented and Godly sons and am the grandmother of a curious and outgoing four-year-old. About the time our grandson was born, our Lord introduced our family into a season of loss and suffering which has continued. However difficult, I know He is there and has a loving purpose.

Over the years God's call has led into other varied roles which have included pastor's wife, published writer of articles and features, editor of a Christian newsmagazine, secondary English teacher in public school for over twenty years, and a volunteer in ministry efforts and civic affairs that support healthy community. Since my retirement from full-time employment, I've rediscovered time to enjoy my continuing interest in art, photography, music, gardening, and design.

My husband and I share a passion for authentic ministry and discipleship, which God has used to facilitate intimate small group studies, as well as large group workshops. It's true, you can't teach what you haven't learned; and through life's challenges, my Rock, Sustainer, and Friend has used His presence, His Word, and His body to comfort and grow us in ways we couldn't have imagined.